Let's Eat Lunch

Learning About Picture Graphs

Susan Vaughan

Math for the REAL World™

Rosen Classroom Books & Materials
New York

What is for lunch today?

Two of us eat sandwiches.

Five of us eat pizza.

One of us eats a hot dog.

Three of us eat soup.

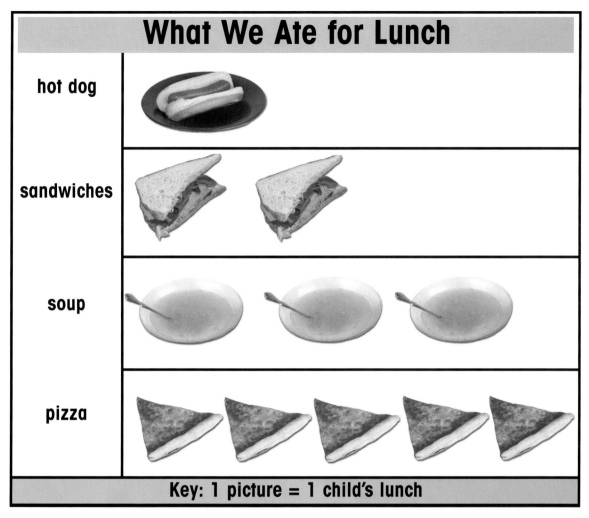

What We Ate for Lunch

hot dog	
sandwiches	
soup	
pizza	

Key: 1 picture = 1 child's lunch

This is what we ate for lunch today!

Words to Know

hot dog

lunch

pizza

sandwiches

soup